ALL EARS

Written by Anthony Robinson

Ears trap sound.
You have a pair of ears
to help you hear.

Not all ears look alike.

Look at all the different ears.

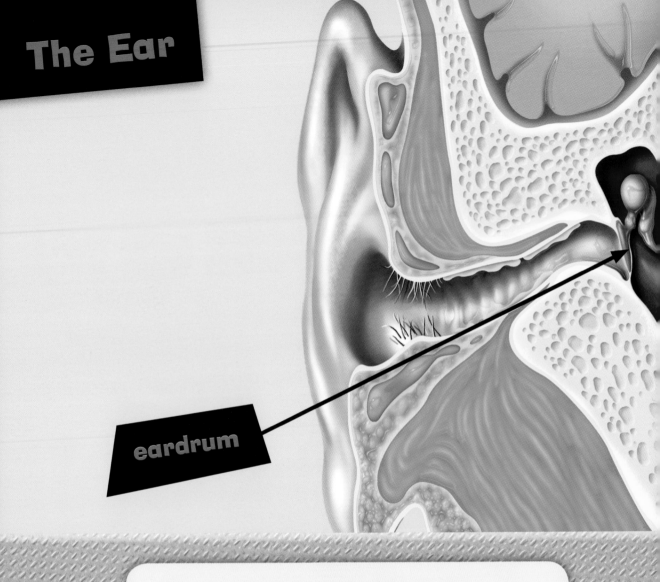

eardrum

Ears trap sounds from the air. The sounds go down the ear and hit the eardrum.

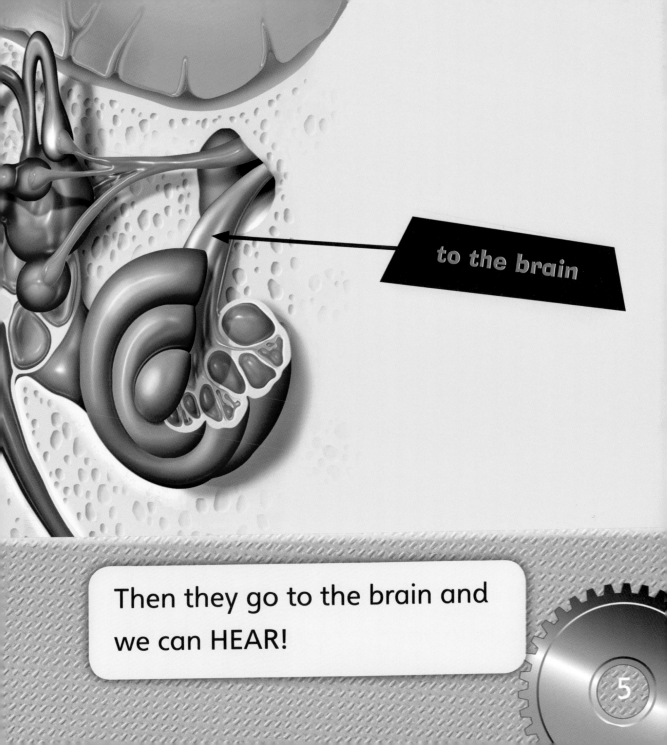

to the brain

Then they go to the brain and we can HEAR!

Ear Facts

hairs

Your ears are joined to your throat. Hairs in your ears stop dust from getting in.

wax

Ears contain goo called wax.
Wax keeps ears soft and moist.

Dogs can hear things we can't hear.
A cat twists its ears to hear sounds
all around.

Can you see ears on the animals here?
No! Fish and serpents are different.
They **feel** the sounds around them.

Ears never rest.

They hear sounds as you sleep!

Did you hear that earwigs
live in ears?
That is pure rubbish.
They do not!

Remember! Keep your ears clear.
Do not stick things in them.
Ouch!